For my family and friends, and all those who have lived and loved the Tasmanian life.

Alice Hanke :)

Tasmania – a living journey
First published in 2004 by
Alice Hansen
Hobart, Tasmania, Australia.

National Library of Australia
Cataloguing-in-Publication data:
Hansen, Alice.
Tasmania : a living journey.
    ISBN 0 646 44309 7
    1. Tasmania – Description
    and travel – Pictorial works. I.
Tasmania – a living journey.
    919.46

Produced in Tasmania, Australia
Graphic design: Lea Crosswell
Editing: Impress: clear communication
Pre-press: Photolith Reprographics
Printing: PMP Print

FOREWORD

As a young child, little did I know that I was being raised in one of the most pristine, delightful corners of the earth. Not until I reached adult years and was whisked away to the other side of the world did I come to fully appreciate our island home. The vastness of our space, the vibrant colours of our landscape, and the character of our people combine to create a unique haven.

This is a place where the air is at its purest. Where nature is at its finest. And where life is at its most carefree. Here, people still have time for others and the pace of life has not yet swallowed up the journey of living.

It is with passion and a vision for our future that I have compiled a small sample of our rich culture and breathtaking scenery. Photographs taken by local artists and gripping quotes from Tasmanians themselves allow the spirit of the people to shine vibrantly. My intention was to capture a living moment in Tasmania's history, complete with its ancient forests and the people who roam them today.

Through a combination of words and pictures it is possible to paint a portrait of Tasmania as we know it. As spoken by those who have chosen to live their lives here, it offers a compelling tribute to a much-loved homeland. That a small piece of land evokes such pride and emotion indicates we have landed somewhere special. While this tiny state has become a sought-after holiday destination, Tasmanians will say that the true beauty of our island lies in her daily life.

Hidden from the rest of the world, Tasmania remains a place of untouched beauty – a region where, even today, remote areas are yet to feel the touch of humanity's hand. There are few places left on the planet where this privilege is enjoyed. To stand on a remote beach, the cool sand between your toes and the fresh sea breeze against your face, is to know that you are truly one with this faraway land.

Wherever Tasmanians roam, a quiet whisper reminds us where we hail from. Within our minds we set aside an image of home. It is the place that all others are compared with, the place of our birth. This island's magnetic personality gently draws home again all those who have left her shores. In a strange way, Tasmania is a nurturing mother, shaping each of us into the people we become.

This small honouring of Tasmania feels inadequate considering all that she has offered to me. It is near impossible to squeeze into a few pages the majesty and beauty of the place. I hope, however, that it offers insight into a land separated from the rest of the world through the glory of its wild landscape and the soul of its people. Tasmania may sometimes be left off the global map; perhaps it's because this small island has a presence that can never be fully defined on paper. I trust that you will enjoy this living journey.

Alice Hansen

*66 It would be vain of me to attempt to describe my feelings
when I beheld this lonely harbour lying at the world's end,
separated as it were from the rest of the universe – 'twas nature
and nature in her wildest mood... 99*

Admiral Bruni D'Entrecasteaux

The beauty of Tasmania can be found when one comes right up close to nature and meets it face to face. It is then that the fine detail and intricate delicacy can be fully realised.

Margate

66 *Tasmania sits patiently, waiting to be explored. It is nature's playground, anticipating the scurry of excited feet. For the adventurous spirit in all of us, this splendid island is a wandering wonderland.* 99

Bellerive

A small dot on the world map, yet so exquisite to the eye. Let the secret remain our own.

Kempton

"Tasmania is all about play. Here you are free
to do as you wish. For as long as you want.
Leave no stone unturned."

Kings Meadows

"Waves crash hard into the Tasmanian coast –
awesome, relentless waves heaving in from the
ocean, powered by the surge of winds from
distant lands."

Rosebery

"Tasmanian waters can be unforgiving and powerful.
Watching giant waves crashing into coastal rocks
you can almost feel the shore's pain. But for those
brave and willing, this angry sea can offer some of
the greatest surfing in the country."

Smithton

66 *Immersed in the wilderness, tackling a steep rocky ascent, we sense we are not alone. A quiet rustling from a nearby bush confirms our suspicion. A furry head takes a good long look at us before bounding away into the bushes. These inquisitive little wallabies scatter themselves along the entire eight hour walk to the plateau, reminding us that we are merely visitors to their domain.* 99

Cygnet

66 *Our native animals are wild and free, displaying an untamed instinct that is deep in the heart of all Tasmanians.* 99

Zeehan

66 *If heaven were a place on Earth I am convinced that Tasmania would claim the title. It's a small drop of paradise at the end of the world that some of us are fortunate enough to live and breathe every single day.* 99

Hobart

❝ There are no words that can fully describe the beauty of the Tasmanian landscape. The rays of light dance on the mountain faces and through the trees in a way that makes you wish you could wander through the wilderness forever. ❞

Sorell

"Across the globe, in magazines and on travel documentaries, Tasmania has been hailed as the best temperate island in the world; why would we ever want to leave?"

Hobart

66 *I love the people of Tasmania – genuine, natural and laid back. What you see is what you get down here in Tassie.* 99

Lindisfarne

66 *Every Saturday morning touristy feet bustle through Salamanca Market by the thousands, awakening the city of Hobart. From paintings to wind instruments, creative flair sweeps through the stalls and charms the visitors.* 99

Kingston

66 *What do I love about living in Tasmania? No question, the lifestyle. There is no other place on Earth that offers an approach to life that is so effortless and carefree. It is this spirit within our people that makes Tasmania the perfect place to live.* 99

Georgetown

Wynyard

"From ancient landscapes to modern society, Tasmania offers it all – rugged mountains and impenetrable wilderness; fine local wines and cheeses. It is the perfect blend of days gone by and an exciting tomorrow."

Launceston

It is not until you stand atop the lookout beholding magnificent Wineglass Bay that you are truly overcome by the beauty of the natural world. The crystal blue water rolls up to the glistening sand in a gentle crescent formed by the tides of nature. Absolutely mesmerising.

St Helens

"I will never forget wandering down onto Wineglass Bay and seeing, just beyond the overhanging foliage, an inquisitive little wallaby. I had never seen such a sight – a beach wallaby standing by to welcome us into his domain. Instead of bounding away he patiently sat and even enjoyed a few strokes on the head; what a friendly companion we had come across! It is times like these that make Tasmania a delightful place to live."

Latrobe

" The cascading waterfalls embody the spirit of the Tasmanian people. The water tumbles with unleashed freedom, reflecting our inborn instinct to wander freely where we choose. "

Invermay

" For those of us who love to explore there is no place like Tasmania. Its trails stretch as far as your imagination will take you. It's a magical place. A special place. Despite its tiny size, Tasmania takes a lifetime to discover and appreciate completely. "

Beaconsfield

It would seem that people in the rest of the world are travelling along at such an incredible pace that the scenery around them becomes a blur. I love the fact that here in Tassie we are able to stop and marvel at the gifts we have, rather than rush by without noticing.

Swansea

"Tasmanian life can be summed up in one word: simplicity. No whistles and bells for us, we like it just the way it is. We find comfort in the steadiness and simplicity of the quiet life."
New Town

"There is a stillness in the early morning as the mist rises off the river. It's a time of the day where the silence is magic and the tranquillity is captivating. It's a time when the rest of the world is yet to awaken to the beauty of a brand new Tasmanian morning. I love to sit, and watch, and wait for it to flourish into a brand new day."
Huon Valley

66 *A whole new brilliance can be seen when snow covers the Tasmanian highlands. Our family used to stay in a modest old hut with an inviting open fire in the Cradle Mountain area. I loved the feeling of being curled up in my sleeping bag and opening my eyes to the sight of snow drifting past the quaint window beside me. It's one of those moments that stay with you for a lifetime.* 99

Berriedale

66 *There is something very original about the Tasmanian landscape. Even blanketed in deep snow, there are still unique qualities that remind us where we are – rich blue skies and bold, tall gum trees rising up from the white earth.* 99

Shearwater

Explore. Learn. Discover. Imagine. Cherish.

Coles Bay

"When we leave Tasmania and return, we are able to see the beauty of what we have here and appreciate the lifestyle. Why would we want to live anywhere else?"

Relbia

66 Behold the Walls of Jerusalem! Welcome to a small patch of heaven atop a quiet plateau in Tasmania. To enter the park is to enter a new world – rich with the colour of wild flowers, brimming with underground creeks meandering their way beneath your heavy boots, and glowing with a warm sunlight that brings the mountain walls to life around you. 99

Blackmans Bay

Where Tasmania takes you is up to you. Prepare to immerse yourself in her rich and colourful personality.

Deloraine

"I have wandered the Tasmanian wilderness
for many years now, and it never ceases to
amaze me. Every turn of the trail offers a new
gift to the eye. It is a place that you could never
grow tired of exploring. As long as my legs
will carry me, I will continue to discover new
secrets of this land."

Legana

"Flowing gently, the river meanders its way
down the mountain side with swift turns and
tender curves. It knows its destination, but plays
the journey for all it's worth."

East Devonport

66 *Setting foot and becoming immersed in a temperate Tasmanian rainforest is like slipping back into ancient times. The moist, cool air pressing lightly on your skin and the trickle of a nearby creek ignite the senses and allow the outside world to drift away.* 99

Derwent Park

"To explore territory where perhaps no human being has walked before is a special experience. Wandering into the wilderness of southwestern Tasmania leaves much in the hands of nature and a lonely compass."

West Hobart

66 *Tasmania does not need to try. Its captivating grandeur enriches the soul.* 99

Sandy Bay

66 *Tasmania offers anyone with a taste for adventure a magnificent arena to bound through. Grown up children from across the state paddle through waters, wander deeper into caves, and clamber higher up mountains – all for the exhilarating reward of having met the challenge.* 99

Sheffield

66 *Where earth and sea collide is a beautiful thing. Where the ocean meets Tasmanian shores, this collision has never been sweeter.* 99

Longford

66 Tasmania will take you to places as far as your imagination can see. And if you cannot imagine, it will create for you scenery beyond your dreams. 99

Lauderdale

"Wind-swept sand dunes remind us of the ever changing environment, of generations that have passed and of generations to come. The wind is carried on the hands of time, and with change, new sand arrives."

Burnie

"From the countryside to the majestic coastline. From the wineries to the world-class cuisine. From the thick wilderness to the space of far stretching beaches. This is Tasmania. This is why I live here and this is what I love."

Devonport

Down by the shore of Hobart is the perfect place for friends to meet and relax. The gently rocking boats, the vast waters and magnificent Mount Wellington compete for your gaze while you sit and sip on your after-work drinks.

Hobart

"Tasmanians are eager, warm and friendly.
They have chosen to live a life where the world
takes a little more care, and time is not always
of the essence. They want to learn about you,
make you feel comfortable, and most of all,
they want you to stay awhile."

Bridgewater

"One might think that distance and separation
have caused Tasmania to fall behind in the realm
of culinary delights, but this tiny island has a few
exquisite secrets of her own. Beautifully crafted
wines and fine gourmet foods have come
naturally to the 'natural state' and continue to
satisfy even the most worldly of visitors."

East Launceston

66 *The creation of Tasmania has left us with nature's finest collection of splendid landscapes – all within the small space of a tiny island. It is not uncommon to be bathing at the beach in the morning and marvelling at the wild flowers in the mountains by the afternoon.* 99

Rosny

66 *No matter where you live on this little island, there is a patch of paradise set aside for all. During the summer months, little beaches across the island are scattered with eager young surf lifesavers, learning the ropes and keeping a watchful eye on the splashing toddlers. There's a real community feel down by Tasmanian shores, it's a place where mothers can relax and families may gather.* 99

Boat Harbour

"When we reach the pinnacle, that's when Tasmania rewards us."

Kettering

"Natural lakes abound in the highland areas of Tasmania, offering world class fly-fishing venues and breathtaking scenery. With grand mountainous backdrops, these lakes glisten with pride and beauty."

Exeter

"When I am up at the lakes fly-fishing I enter a new dimension. It's a different world up there – one of serenity, of quiet thought and of tranquil surroundings. I can become lost in my own thoughts for days on end."

Hobart

66 *The crumbling walls of Port Arthur hold within them a history as deep and rich as our vast landscape.* 99

Rokeby

"Tasmania is breathing with the history of years gone by. Richmond Bridge, the oldest bridge in Australia, is a lasting testament to those who constructed her. The quaint historic towns that line the central highways are alive with tales of early Tasmanian inhabitancy."

Hawley

Just when one might think the island of Tasmania has all its beauty wrapped within its shores, there on the horizon sits a fascinating afterthought – Maria Island. This tiny island, with sandstone cliffs and sweeping hills, is enchanting.

Latrobe

Tasmania – a long way from the rest of the world.

Oatlands

"I think Tasmanian lighthouses have the best view of all. Sitting upon rugged coastlines and beautiful points, they enjoy a panoramic view of natural brilliance that stretches out beyond the reaches of their shining light."

Battery Point

Details of credits as follows:

Page 5: Tasman Peninsula, view south from Waterfall Bluff at sunrise
Photographer: G. Murray

Page 6: Twisted Lakes, Cradle Mountain-Lake St Clair National Park
Photographer: K. Nunn

Page 7: Pandani and tarn, Cradle Mountain-Lake St Clair National Park
Photographer: R. Blakers

Page 9: Myrtle, Walls of Jerusalem National Park
Photographer: R. Blakers

Page 10: Remarkable Cave, Tasman Peninsula
Photographer: K. Nunn

Page 11: Cloudy Bay, Bruny Island
Photographer: G. Murray

Page 13: Wallabies at Cradle Mountain-Lake St Clair National Park
Photographer: S. Lovegrove

Page 14: Freycinet National Park
Photographer: S. Lovegrove

Page 16: Old path, north Cradle Mountain area
Photographer: S. Lovegrove

Page 17: Cradle Mountain and Dove Lake, Cradle Mountain-Lake St Clair National Park
Photographer: G. Murray

Page 18: Salamanca Market, Hobart
Photographer: S. Lovegrove

Page 20: Princes Park, Battery Point, Hobart
Photographer: S. Lovegrove

Page 21: Tulips, Table Cape
Photographer: G. Murray

Page 22: Wineglass Bay, Freycinet National Park
Photographer: G. Murray

Page 23: Wineglass Bay, Freycinet National Park
Photographer: G. Murray

Page 25: Russell Falls, Mount Field National Park
Photographer: G. Murray

Page 26: Hut near Gordon River, Franklin-Gordon Wild Rivers National Park
Photographer: S. Lovegrove

Page 27: Rowing, Macquarie Harbour
Photographer: S. Lovegrove

Page 29: Waldheim Chalet, Cradle Mountain-Lake St Clair National Park
Photographer: J. Fairhall

Page 30: Ocean Beach at sunset, Strahan
Photographer: S. Lovegrove

Page 31: Rock formation, Tasman Peninsula
Photographer: S. Lovegrove

Page 33: Walls of Jerusalem National Park
Photographer: S. Lovegrove

Page 34: Marriotts Falls, near Mount Field
Photographer: G. Murray

Page 35: Tasmanian devil resting
Photographer: S. Lovegrove

Page 36: Pandani and myrtle in rainforest on Mount Anne, Southwest National Park
Photographer: G. Murray

Page 37: Cushion plant, North East Ridge, Mount Anne, Southwest National Park
Photographer: G. Murray

Page 38: Freycinet National Park
Photographer: R. Blakers

Page 40: Henty Dunes, west coast of Tasmania
Photographer: G. Murray

Page 41: Jetty at sunset, Freycinet Lodge, Freycinet National Park
Photographer: G. Murray

Page 42: Sunrise on Derwent River, Hobart
Photographer: S. Lovegrove

Page 43: Outdoor café, Salamanca, Hobart
Photographer: S. Lovegrove

Page 45: Boat Harbour beach
Photographer: G. Murray

Page 46: Lake Oberon, Western Arthur Range, Southwest National Park
Photographer: G. Murray

Page 48: Church, Port Arthur
Photographer: S. Lovegrove

Page 49: Richmond Bridge
Photographer: S. Lovegrove

Page 50: Painted Cliffs, Maria Island National Park
Photographer: G. Murray

Page 52: Bluestone Bay, Freycinet National Park
Photographer: K. Nunn

Page 53: Eddystone Point Lighthouse, Mount William National Park
Photographer: J. Fairhall

Page 56: Snow gums, Mount Field National Park
Photographer: G. Murray

Alice Hansen was born and raised in Devonport, Tasmania. After completing high school she spent five years in the United States pursuing a tennis scholarship and university degree. Alice returned to Australia in January 2004 and now resides in Hobart.

A special thank you to Lea Crosswell, Adrian Edwards, Alan Waugh, Suzanne Cooper, Bruce Ransley, Dean Jackson and to all those Tasmanians who offered their beautiful words.

King Island

BASS STRAIT

Flinders Island

TASMANIA

Stanley
Smithton
Burnie
Ulverstone
Devonport
George Town
Scottsdale
Sheffield
St Helens
Waratah
Launceston
Scamander
Savage River
Deloraine
Longford
St Marys
Rosebery
Tullah
Zeehan
Campbell Town
Bicheno
Queenstown
Strahan
Swansea
Coles Bay
Tarraleah
Oatlands
Ouse
Hamilton
Orford
Richmond
Maria Island
HOBART
Huonville
Geeveston
Port Arthur
Dover
Bruny Island

AUSTRALIA